A TREASURE OF MEASURES

Mike Downs

Joy Hwang Ruiz

chronicle books·san francisco

Ticks of a clock measure **seconds** of time.

Marks on a ruler show **inches** of line.

Ounces on scales reveal a weight.

Calendars measure the **year** by each date.

The measures of science are very precise,
each counted or marked with the proper device.
But how about getting some measuring done
in ways that are wildly, wonderfully fun?

We rush through our lives in our cars and in planes,
on bicycles, sailboats, scooters, and trains.
Miles per hour can tell us our speed,
but what other measures could cover this need?

On boats, we might count every snap of the sail;
on trains, every clank on the clattering rail.
On planes, view the landscape that's drifting below.
On bikes, feel the *whooshing* of wind as we go!

A flurry of raindrops erupts from the sky!
A drizzle? Or is it a storm passing by?
Decibels capture each rainy day's sound,
but what other measures of rain can be found?

Let's count all the glistening, silvery drops
and measure each puddle with skips and with hops.
We'll watch the umbrellas that snap into view
or measure the squish of a waterlogged shoe.

From bustling traffic to countryside lanes,
our travels can take us through forests and plains.
Highway signs measure this distance in **miles**,
but why not in bridges or horses or smiles?

Let's measure our trip by the scents on the breeze
or count every curve as we steer through the trees.

We'll savor each laugh we enjoy on the way
at goofy surprises that brighten our day.

Nothing delights like the joy of a book
when reading together, curled up in a nook.
Minutes fly by with each flip of a page,
but stories hold so many ways to engage!

We'll measure our time
by the tales that unfold,
the menacing monsters,
the searches for gold.
By each roar of laughter,
by each tear we cry,
by each cheer for heroes
who soar through the sky.

The mightiest branch begins life as a twig.
The tiniest child grows from little to big.
Each **year** we mark **inches** of growth on the wall,
but growing means much more than just getting tall!

Mary
1981

Mary
1977

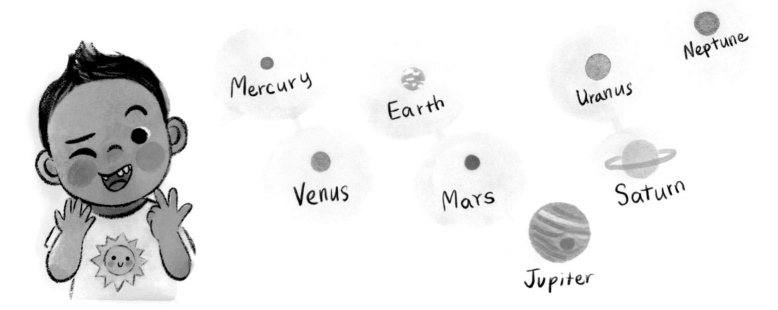

How much have we grown? We can measure in reach
or by counting new words that we use in our speech.
In how far we jump, in how high we swing,
in how we approach what tomorrow will bring.

Look to the heavens, toward Venus or Mars,
and gaze at the flashes of twinkling stars.
Lumens describe every shimmer of light,
but what other measures appear in the night?

Let's count every planet aglow in the dark
or seek constellations that flicker and spark.
We'll find our own star, whether giant or small,
a wished-upon star that shines brightest of all!

Our lives are a treasure
we measure in **years**,
but why not in friendships
or laughter or cheers?

Or . . .

birthday parties, flying kites, funny movies, starry nights.

Walking puppies, catching bugs, roller coasters, joyful hugs.

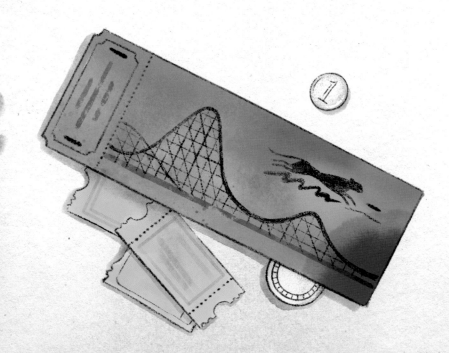

Sidewalk hopscotch, hide-and-seek, skipping stones across a creek.

Sleeping over, playing cards, football games in grassy yards.

Playing soccer, riding bikes,
beaches, kayaks, taking hikes.
Summer campouts, fireflies,
cotton candy, fond goodbyes.

Our lives overflow with these magical measures
and moments of wonder to cherish as treasures.
So open your eyes and your heart and your mind . . .
Imagine the marvelous measures you'll find!

SYSTEMS OF MEASUREMENT

Measuring can be confusing! Since ancient times, people have invented different units of measurement in different parts of the world. In ancient Egypt, the distance from a person's elbow to their wrist or to the tip of their middle finger was a **cubit**. (As you might guess, this measure was not always exact.) A **foot** was another measure that could change. It could be anywhere from 10 inches to 14 inches, depending on which society, or even which area, you were from. Over the years, having so many different measurement systems became a problem.

Today, there are two primary systems of measurement: the British Imperial System and the metric system. The British Imperial System contains a mishmash of measures developed over hundreds of years. Only a few countries in the world still use this system, including the United States of America, Myanmar, and Liberia. Even the British are beginning to switch from their original system of measurement to the metric system, which measures things in multiples of ten.

Here is a simple example of the different ways each system measures distance:

British Imperial System

1 yard = 3 feet   (about $\frac{9}{10}$ of a metre)

1 mile = 1,760 yards   (about $1\frac{3}{5}$ kilometres)

Metric System

1 metre = 100 centimetres   (about $3\frac{3}{10}$ feet)

1 kilometre = 1,000 metres   (about $\frac{3}{5}$ of a mile)

These are just some examples of the many scientific units of measurement we use to understand our world. They are useful and very important! But it is just as important to find your own ways to observe the incredible world that surrounds us, every single day. Keep your eyes wide open, use your imagination, and see if you can invent some wonderful measures of your own!

UNITS OF MEASUREMENT IN THIS BOOK AND BEYOND

Ounces and pounds are measures of weight.

- 1 ounce is about the weight of 11 pennies or 10 Ping-Pong balls.
- 1 pound is equal to 16 ounces. *That's about 55 gumballs or 20 puffy cones of cotton candy!*

A decibel is a measure of sound.

- 30 decibels is the volume of a whisper. *Try whispering "May I have some ice cream, please?"*
- 60 decibels is your normal speaking volume. *Now say "Thank you for the ice cream" in your regular voice.*
- 120 decibels is the volume of a siren. *It's also about the volume of the world's loudest shout! If you yelled "That ice cream was SO good!" your shout would probably be about 80 to 110 decibels.*

A lumen is a measure of light.

- 50 lumens is as bright as a beaming night-light. *It is also roughly as bright as 2,000 fireflies all shining at the same time.*
- 1,100 lumens is as bright as a standard overhead light. *With a flashlight this bright, you could see all the way across 2 soccer fields at night—and maybe even a little farther!*

Inches, feet, and yards are measures of distance.

- Distance can be measured in any direction. When you measure height, you are measuring a vertical distance!
- 1 foot is equal to 12 inches. *That's about the length of 2 ostrich eggs placed end to end.*
- 1 yard is equal to 3 feet. *That's around the height of the world's tallest female Great Dane!*

A **mile** is a measure of distance.

- Miles measured on land are also known as statute miles.
- 1 mile is equal to 5,280 feet or about 17½ football fields. *That's also about the length of 6,400 pieces of spaghetti placed end to end or 15,800 monarch butterflies flying wing tip to wing tip.*

Minutes and **hours** are measures of time.

- 1 minute is equal to 60 seconds. *A minute is long enough to say "Please read this book again" about 30 times.*
- 1 hour is equal to 60 minutes. *An hour is long enough to read this book 5 times!*

Miles per hour is a measure of speed.

- A speedy snail might zip along at 0.03 miles per hour. *That's 1 mile in 33⅓ hours (more than 1⅓ days)!*
- A supersonic jet flying at the speed of sound—about 770 miles per hour—would travel around the world 1 time while the snail finished traveling that 1 mile!

Days, months, and **years** are measures of time.

- 1 day is equal to 24 hours. *This is how long it takes Earth to spin around on its axis 1 full time.*
- 1 month is equal to either 30 or 31 days (except for the month of February). *February is usually 28 days long. But every 4 years, February gets an extra day, so it has 29 days! That year is called a leap year.*
- 1 year is equal to 365 days (except for leap years). *A leap year has 366 days, and it has nothing to do with jumping! It happens once every 4 years. Why? Because Earth doesn't circle the sun in exactly 365 days. Its orbit takes 365 days plus a little bit more, about an extra ¼ of a day. This means that we need to add an extra day to our calendars once every 4 years to keep them correct!*

LET'S MEASURE TOGETHER!

Measuring SOUND

Stand on one side of a room. Ask a friend to stand on the other side of the room.

- **Whisper:** Say "Please give me a high five" very quietly. If they run over to give you a high five, then your voice was louder than a whisper!

- **Normal Voice:** Say "Please turn around three times and touch your toes." If they follow your instructions, then your normal speaking voice was just the right volume. If they don't do it, either you are whispering or your friend doesn't want to turn around three times and touch their toes!

- **Yelling Voice:** Do NOT yell. Yelling inside the house is a very bad idea. But you can use a normal speaking volume to say "I am not yelling."

Measuring DISTANCE

Find a measuring tape or a ruler.

- Place your foot flat on the ground. Use the measuring tape or ruler to measure the length of your foot. *The world's largest human foot ever measured was more than 18 inches long! How close is your foot to the largest human foot ever measured?*

- Stand with your feet together, and mark your starting place. Take a big hop forward, then mark where you ended. Measure the length of your hop. *Each jackrabbit hop is about 5 to 10 feet. How does your hop compare?*

- Lie down, then ask a friend to carefully measure from your feet to your head. This distance tells you how tall you are! *Adult male giraffes can grow to about 18 feet tall. How tall are you compared to a giraffe?*

Measuring SPEED

Find a timer, and ask a friend to help you measure time in seconds.

- Start the timer, then read the tongue twisters below. Stop the timer as soon as you finish.

  Dogs chase frogs on logs in bogs. Cats wear hats and bats eat gnats. Bongo Bear wears underwear and eats a pear while combing hair. If reading these sentences took you

  - 20 seconds: You are reading at a speed of 75 words per minute.

  - 10 seconds: You are reading at a speed of 150 words per minute.

  - Under 10 seconds: You are reading REALLY fast!

- Measure out 50 feet, marking your starting and ending points. Time how long it takes to run from one point to the other. If running 50 feet took you

  - 10 seconds: You ran about as fast as a large cockroach.

  - 5 seconds: You ran about as fast as a mouse.

  - 1 second: You ran about as fast as a startled deer. Wow!

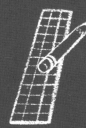

For Amelia—my amazing, talented daughter;
fellow adventurer; and wonderful human being.
Thank you for patiently waiting 20 years. —M. D.

For my Juan, two and three. —J. H. R.

Library of Congress Cataloging-in-Publication Data available.

ISBN 978-1-7972-1215-9

Manufactured in China.

Design by Sara Gillingham Studio.
Typeset in Embury and hand-lettered by Jiae Hwang.
The illustrations in this book were rendered in ink and pencil and colored digitally.

10 9 8 7 6 5 4 3 2 1

Chronicle books and gifts are available at special quantity discounts to corporations,
professional associations, literacy programs, and other organizations. For details and discount information,
please contact our premiums department at corporatesales@chroniclebooks.com or at 1-800-759-0190.

Chronicle Books LLC
680 Second Street
San Francisco, California 94107

Chronicle Books—we see things differently.

Become part of our community at www.chroniclekids.com.